A Gift from Winklesea

Take Part Series

A Gift from Winklesea

Adapted by Sheila Lane and Marion Kemp

from the story by Helen Cresswell

Ward Lock Educational Co. Ltd.

Ward Lock Educational Co Ltd
BIC LIng Kee House
1 Christopher Road
East Grinstead
West Sussex RH19 3BT

A member of the Ling Kee Group
Hong Kong • Singapore • London • New York

A GIFT FROM WINKLESEA

This adaptation published by Ward Lock Educational 1998
© Sheila Lane and Marion Kemp 1998
Cover and text illustrations by Sally Robson

First published - 1998

ISBN 0 7062 5359 0

All rights reserved. No part of this publication may be reproduced, stored in a retrieval system, or transmitted, in any form or by any means, electronic, mechanical, photocopying, recording or otherwise, without the prior written permission of the Publisher.

Printed in Hong Kong

Contents

1	Stone or Egg?	*9*
2	Two Weeks Later	*12*
3	That Evening	*17*
4	What is IT?	*20*
5	Winkie Grows	*25*
6	Getting Ready for the Pet Show	*30*
7	At the Pet Show	*35*
8	Well done, Winkie	*44*
9	Trouble for Winkie	*48*
10	More Trouble	*54*
11	A Big Problem	*56*
12	Winkie Settles It	*59*

★ This sign means that you can make the sounds which go with the story.

Here are the people who take part:

Dad (Mr Kane)

Mum (Mrs Kane)

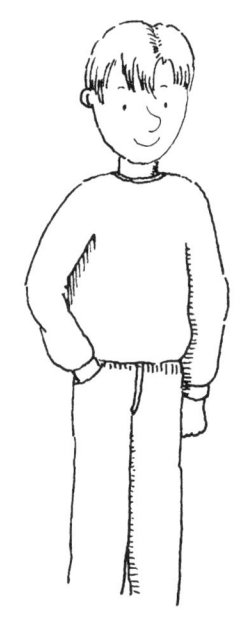

Dan Kane

Mary Kane

Dan and Mary go on a trip to the seaside. At the end of the day they go to the Gift Shop to buy a present for their Mum.

What do Dan and Mary buy?
Read the story and find out.

1 Stone or Egg?

Dan and Mary buy a present for their Mum. It is a greenish blue stone egg, with gold letters on its stand.

Dan The egg looks just right between the clock and the cat.

Dad It's a funny hen that laid THAT egg.

Mary It's not a REAL egg, Dad.

Mum He knows that, Mary.

Dad Anyway, I've never seen an egg with gold letters on its stand.

Mary But I told you, Dad.
It's not a real egg.

Dad   Shall I give it a tap? You never know! Something might hatch out.

Mum   Like what?

Dad   Like a chicken!

Dan   Well, the chicken that comes out of that egg will need a sharp beak.

Mary   Stop it! All of you!
It's not a REAL egg.

Mum   It's very pretty, Mary. What did the lady in the shop say about it?

Mary   She told us where she got it from.

Dad   And where was that?

Dan   She said she saw it lying on the beach at Winklesea and when she picked it up she thought it was an egg.

Mary   I keep telling you!
It's not a REAL egg.

Mum   Well, it looks like an egg to me.

Dan   I asked the lady in the shop if it would break.

Mum   What did she say?

Dan   She rapped it with her pen. Then she said, "It's a stone all right."

Dad So...it's a stone egg. Now, I wonder! What kind of animal could have laid an egg like that?

Mary Dad! I told you!

Mum Sh, Mary! He knows you did. He knows what you said.

Dad All the same, it IS a bit strange.

Mary It cost 40 pence ....

Dan ... and 5 pence extra for the box.

Mum Well, I think it's lovely.

Dad And you couldn't have picked anything your Mum would have liked better.

Dan Still! I wonder what people will say when they see it?

Dad I can guess! They'll say it's some kind of egg. You'll see!

What do you think? Is the Gift from Winklesea a stone or an egg?

11

2 Two Weeks Later

*Mary takes the stone egg down from the shelf and feels it.
Dan is making a model aeroplane.★*

Mary   Look at it Dan.
It feels warm.

Dan   What of it? It's over the fireplace, isn't it?

Mary   Yes. But ... the fire isn't on.

Dan   Bring it here.★

Mary   Go on! Put your hand on it.

Dan   Mmm. Yes, it IS warm, but only a bit.

Mary   But Dan, it's a STONE.

Dan   And stones are usually cold.

Mary   You don't think ... you don't think...
that... it will... h...?

Dan HATCH OUT! A STONE! ★ Ho, Ho! It's just a big pebble, that's all.

Mary But it IS warm.

Dan Well, what d'you think's going to hatch out of it? A chicken?

Mary I don't know.

Dan I'll tell you what we'll do. We'll do an experiment.

Mary What's an ...ex...peri...ment?

Dan It's a kind of test.

Mary Oh yes! We have tests at school.

Dan What we'll do is get a REAL stone out of the garden.

Mary A BIG stone like the Gift from Winklesea?

Dan Yes. We'll put it on the shelf next to the other one. Then tomorrow we'll feel them both together.

Mary Do you mean ... TEST them?

Dan Yes, to see if one of them is warmer than the other.

Mary Yes, I see.
I'll go and find a big stone. ★

Dan Make sure it's about the same size as the Gift.

Mary Look Dan! Here's a stone.
It's very cold.

Dan Of course it is. It's been outside in the soil. You'd better give it a wash, or you'll have Mum after you.★

Mary After US! Not just me.

Dan OK, it was my idea. Wash it in soapy water and dry it on the tea towel.

Mary Now I'll put it up on the shelf.. ★

Dan Put it right next to the Gift from Winklesea.

Mary How long will we have to wait?

Dan Mmm! Let me think ...
... till tomorrow.

Mary Come on, Dan! Get up!

Dan Come on *where*?

Mary To feel the eggs. You know! The EGG TEST

Dan The experiment. Oh THAT!

Mary Dan, come on. PLEASE!

Dan. Oh, all right.★

Mary Go on, Dan. YOU do it.

Dan All right. I'll put my hands over the two stones. There! ... Mm... Mm... Mmm...★

Mary What is it, Dan? What's the matter?

Dan It IS warm. The Gift from Winklesea IS warm. You touch it, Mary.

Mary Oh! Oh! OH!
Is it going to hatch out?

Dan Looks like it. But what into?
That's the point. WHAT INTO?

What do you think the egg stone will hatch into?

3 That Evening

The Kane family are eating fish and chips for their supper, with the TV on. ★

Dad   Switch that TV off.

Mary   But Dad ...

Dad   Switch it off! I can't hear myself eat my supper.

Mum   It's only the lady who tells us about soap.

Dan   Here! Have some tomato sauce on your fish, Dad.

Dad   NO! SWITCH ... IT ... OFF!

Dan   All right! All right! I'll do it. ★

Mary   ★ Listen!

Mum   What was that?

Dan   ★ I can hear a tapping sound.

Dad   Where's it coming from?

Mary ★ Listen! It's coming from over there.

Mum   That's right. ★ Over there!

Dan   It's coming from the shelf.

Dad   Let's all get closer and have a look. Now ...SHUSH!

Mary It's coming from the egg.

Mum   Those taps are coming from INSIDE the egg.

Dan   Look at it! ★ It's rocking about.

Dad   It's getting louder now. ★ SHUSH!

Dan   ★ It's jumping up and down and rocking about all over the place. What's happening?

Mum   What's got into it?

Mary	★ The taps are going on ... ★ and on... ★
Dad	I wonder WHY it's jumping about like that.
Mary	Yes! WHY!
Dad	Do you know what I think?
ALL	NO!
Dad	I think it's going to HATCH!
Mum	Hatch! HATCH?
Dad	Looks like it, Mother. There's SOMETHING banging away inside.
Mary	But what can it be?
Dan	Any minute now ... any minute now. Wait for it. It's going to HATCH any minute ...
Dad	We must DO something.
Mum	Yes, DO SOMETHING
Dan	But WHAT?

What will the egg hatch into?

4 What is it?

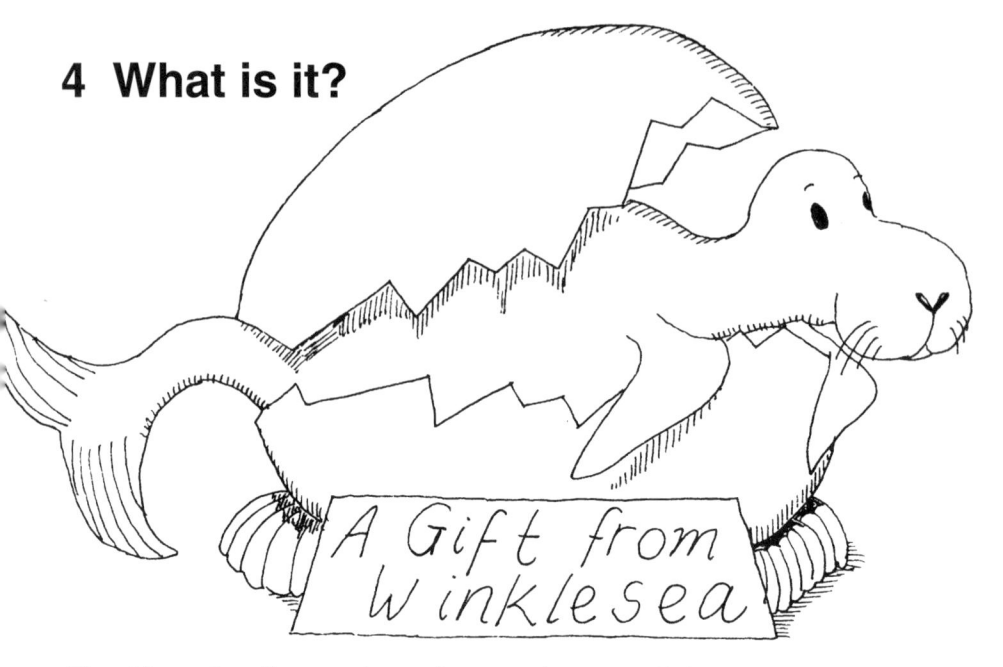

The Kane family watch as the egg jumps off the stand. ★

Dad Shush! All of you! Watch!

Mum Do something someone! Do something!

Dan Quick Dad! Do something!

Dad No! Shush! Let's just watch.

Mary It's a ... It's a ....

Mum But WHAT is it?

Dan It's a ... baby ... kangaroo! Let me look at it. Quick!

Mary No, Dan. Come away.

Mum Dan! Come away from it.

Dad That's right. Come away this minute.

Dan It's all right. It won't bite. Look! You've frightened it now. It's scared of us.

Dad It's gone behind the clock. Well, bless me!

Mary I can just see its head.

Dan It's got a black eye . . . and a grey head . . . and it's sitting there looking at us.

Mary Isn't it sweet?

Mum I don't know about that. I don't think I'd call it sweet.

Dad Well, what's to be done now? That's what I want to know. . . .

Dan Perhaps it's hungry.

Mum Yes, that's it. It's hungry.

Mary Give it a chip, Dan.

Dad That's a good idea. Put the chip on the shelf, Dan. ★

Mary Look! It's coming! ★

Mum It's going to eat that chip.

Dad We'll see. Let's stand here quietly and watch. Well, bless me! It's sniffing round that little chip. ★

Mum   So it IS hungry.

Mary   Look! It's gone!
The chip's gone . . .

Dad   . . . into its great, big mouth.
Well, bless me! That was quick.

Dan   Let's give it another one.

Mum   Yes, give it another chip, Dan.

Mary   Look! ★ It's sniffing again.

Mum   That chip's gone now ... and into its great big mouth.

Mary   Let's give it some more chips. .

Dan   Watch everybody. ★ Its mouth opens and shuts like clockwork.

Mum   Don't give it any more.

Dad   You'll give it indigestion.

Mary   Yes! It's only a baby.

Dan   All right! I suppose it IS only just out of its shell.

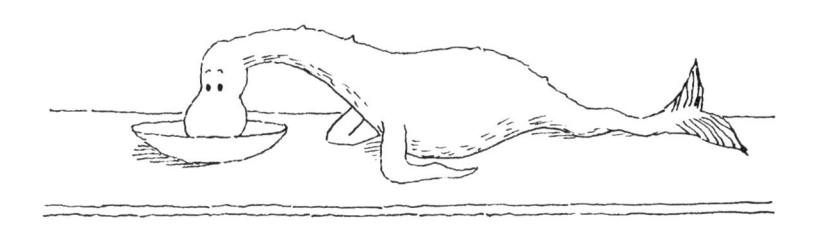

Dad I know! Give it a saucer of milk, Mary. That's more like what it wants.

Mary ★ Here it is.
Come on, little one ... milk ... milk.

Mum Look! ★ It likes milk.

Dad It was milk it wanted ... Well everybody ... the meal's over. So now what?

Mum Where can we put it? That's what I want to know. It can't stay up there.

Dan There's a mouse cage in the loft, Mum.

Mary No! We can't put it into a cage.

Dad I know! The aquarium. It might like being in water.

Mum That's a good idea.

Dan But we might drown it.

Dad No harm in trying it out. It came out of the sea, didn't it?

Dan I'll fetch the aquarium from under the sink.★

Mary Put some water in it. ★

Mum And a stone or two. ★

Dad Now put the Gift down into it ...very gently, mind.

Dan Look at that! It's swimming about. It likes its new home and family.

Dad If it's one of the family, we must give it a proper name.★

Dan Well ... it came from Winklesea ...★

Mary Winklesea ... Winkle WINKIE!
Yes! Let's call HIM ..WINKIE!

Mum WINKIE ... one of OUR family.

But what *is* Winkie?

5 Winkie Grows

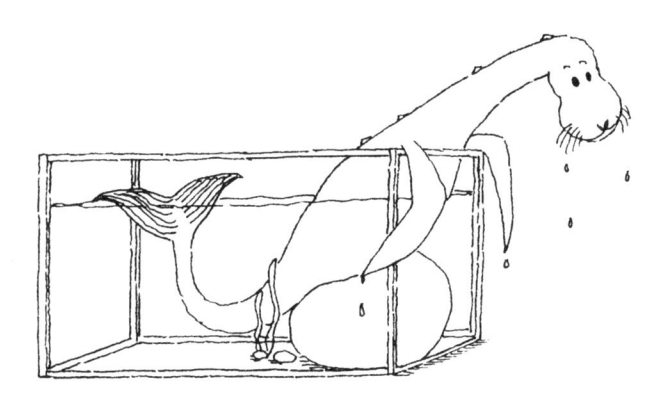

A day or two later the Kane family are eating their supper and talking about Winkie. ★

Mum   Winkie's getting bigger. ...

Mary   ... and bigger ... and BIGGER.

Dad   I reckon he's four times bigger than he was when he came out of that egg. He wouldn't fit into it now.

Dan   Look at him! He can climb up onto his rock and get over the side of the aquarium.

Dad   And then paddle about ... on dry land.

Mum   Yes! On my carpet! Look at his wet feet.

Mary   We can mop up the water, Mum.

Dad   I wish he'd stay in his aquarium.

Mum   Or stay OUT of it.

Dan   Winkie's like a frog. I bet he's an amphibian.

Mary   What's that, Dan?

Dan   It means he can live in the water or on the land.

Dad   Do you mean he's a sea lion?

Dan   No! A sea lion doesn't come out of an egg. Sea lions are mammals ... I think.

Mum   But he looks a bit like a sea lion.

Dan   Well ... he's got whiskers and a pair of flippers.

Dad   His neck's a bit long. He could be a SORT of sea lion.

Mum   If he's a sea lion, he can catch fish in his mouth.

Mary   Like they do at the Zoo.

Dad   We'll try him. We'll try him with a piece of seed cake.

Mary   ★ Come on, sea lion!

Dan   Catch! ★

Mum   ★ Snap! ★ It's gone!

Dad Good gracious!

Mum That was quick!

Mary Let me try ...
Come on sea lion ... ★ CATCH!

Dan It's gone! Quick as lightning.

Dad Well, if Winkie's not a sea lion, he's as clever as one.

Dan And twice as hungry. Give him some more seed cake, Mary.

Mary Come on, sea lion. ★ CATCH!

Mum No, no! Don't give him any more, Mary.

Dad He's as big as a kitten now. I reckon he's grown since I came home from work.

Mum I reckon you can SEE him growing.

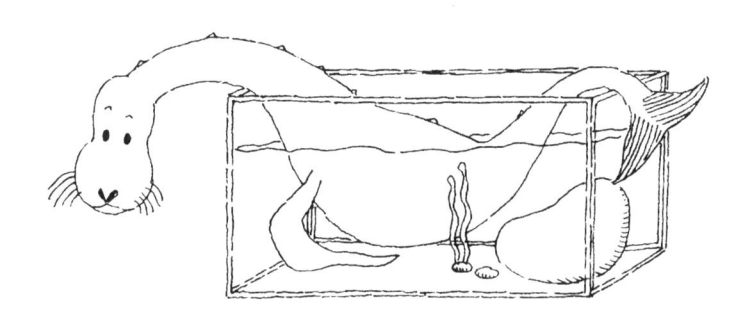

Dan Look! He's trying to get back into his aquarium. But it's a tight squeeze.

27

Dad   I know! There's an old zinc bath in the garden shed. Let's get it out and try Winkie in that. ★

Mum   That's better. ★ He can splash about in this now.

Dan   We can keep it out here on the grass in the daytime.

Mary   Then he can make the grass wet.

Mum   But we must make a bed for him inside at night time.

Mary   Can he have a bed in the kitchen, Mum?

Mum   In my kitchen! Oh ... all right. It will be nice and warm for him in there.

Dan   Yes, we can use the old dog basket that Uncle Fred gave us.

Dad   Talking of Uncle Fred ... he came round yesterday.

Mum   Did he see Winkie, Dad?

Mary   What did he say, Dad?

Dad He said, "That's a rum sort of pet!"

Dan Did he ask where he came from?

Dad He did. And when I told him he said, "Well, I'm blessed! If I was you I would get that pet put away in a Zoo."

Mary In a Zoo!
But he's a pet!

Mum No, we can't put Winkie in a Zoo.

Dad Uncle Fred said that we don't know what he's going to turn into. He said it might be ..

Mary What?

Mum Well what?

Dan WHAT did he say it might be, Dad?

Dad He said, "I reckon, that what you've got there, give or take a yard or two – is a Loch Ness Monster!"

Mum A LOCH NESS MONSTER! Oh dear! Oh dear!

Dan Did you hear that Winkie? Uncle Fred says you might be a Loch Ness Monster.

Mary A Loch Ness Monster!

Dan Look at him everybody. He's smiling!

Do you think that Winkie will turn into a Loch Ness Monster?

6 Getting Ready for the Pet Show

> Children's Pet Show
> Bring your pet along to the church hall by 10am to be judged by Mr. Hunter from the Corner Pet Shop at 11 am.
> EACH PET MUST GO TO THE SHOW IN A PROPER PET CONTAINER.

The Kane family are reading from a printed sheet of paper which Dan has brought home.

Dan   Look at this! It's about a Children's Pet Show.

Mary   A PET SHOW!

Mum   Yes. It says, "Bring your pet along at 10am."

Dad   I know! That will be run by the Vicar in the church hall at the church bazaar.

Dan   Don't you see, everybody? We can try for a prize.

Mary   Dan! Do you mean that we can try for a prize with Winkie?

Dan   Of course! Our Winkie's a pet, isn't he?

Mum   What else does it say on the paper?

Dan   It says, "Bring your pet along to the church hall by 10am to be judged by Mr Hunter from the Corner Pet Shop at 11am."

7 At the Pet Show

The next morning Dan and Mary spend an hour getting Winkie ready for the Pet Show. Then they put him in the wheelbarrow. ★

Dan He looks really beautiful after that shampoo and brush.

Mary Yes, it has made his coat shine in the sun.

Dan But I can't help wondering what people are going to think when they see him going up the road in a wheelbarrow.

Mary Let's go, then we shall find out.

Dan I'll push him. You keep close by the side of the wheelbarrow, Mary.

Mary All right. I'll stay close to him.
Off we go! ★

Dan Here's the main road. ★ I'd better be careful.

Mary Slow down, Dan! ★
SLOW DOWN

Dan I don't think I can.

Mary You must!
YOU MUST!
★ You're going much too FAST!
Slow down, I tell you!!

Dan I'm trying ...but I can't.
Help! ★
The wheel's gone over the kerb now.

Mary It's upset Winkie. ★
Look at him!
He's standing up.

Dan He doesn't like this, not one little bit. Listen to the way he's going, "WHOOP! WHOOP!"

Mary Sit down, Winkie. Sit down!

Dan ★ He's beating his chest now. That shows he's upset. I can't hold the wheelbarrow. ★ Look how it's rocking.

Mary SIT DOWN, WINKIE! PLEASE!

Dan If he falls out, he'll get all dirty again.

Mary PLEASE WINKIE! PLEASE!

Dan I know! I'll let the handles of the wheelbarrow fall down. ★ THERE!

Mary Good! But look!

Dan All those people ...

Dan Look at the people!
They're shouting at Winkie.

"It'll want a licence."

"It ought to be in a cage."

Mary Come on! Come on! Let's get to the Church Hall. ★

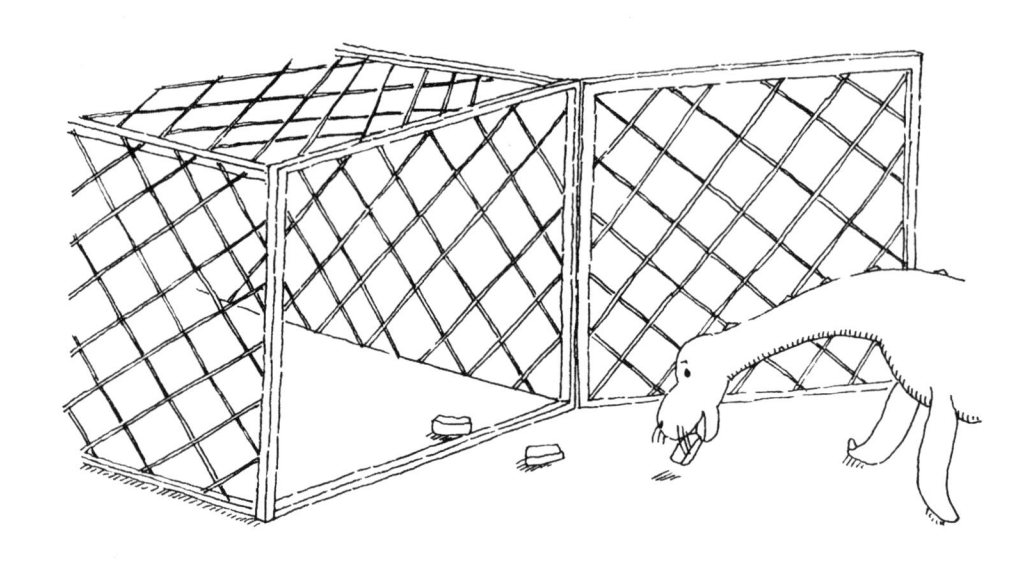

Dan We'll leave the wheelbarrow outside and lead Winkie to the cage with a trail of biscuits.★

Mary Yes, come on, Winkie ... Winkie!..Winkie! .... Come on ... Come on...★.
In you go! ...Good! ★

Dan ★ I'll whip the netting across.
That's it! He's in! He's caged.

Mary Oh Dan! I can't bear seeing him in that cage.

Dan I can't either. But it's not for long.

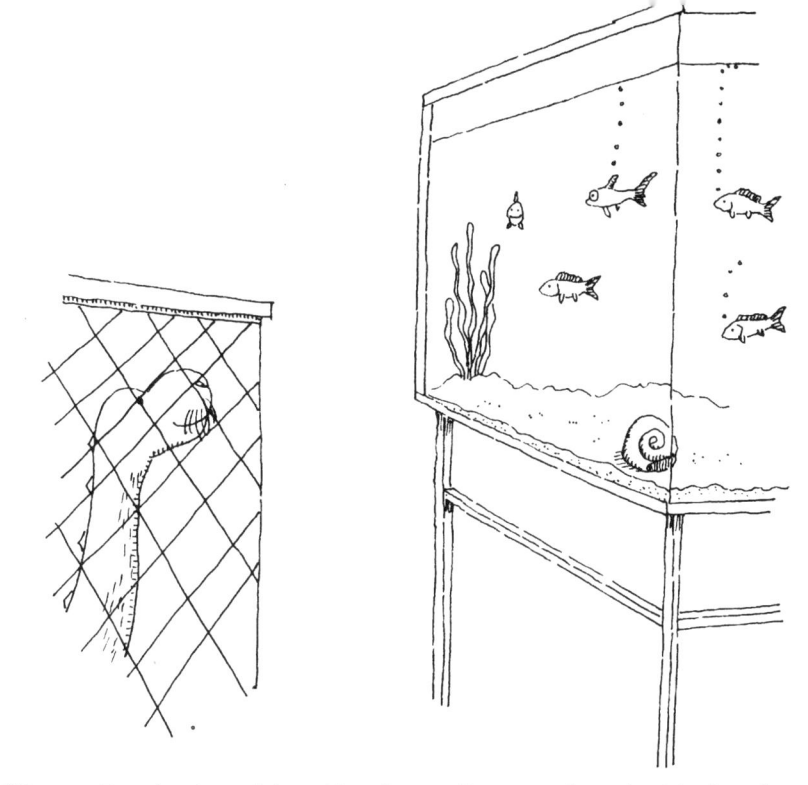

Mary But look at him. He doesn't seem to mind being in his cage now.

Dan No, he doesn't. Well I'm blessed! ★ He's giving little leaps up and down and staring at something.

Mary Look at him now.

Dan ★ He's whimpering and scrabbling at the wire netting. What's he staring at?

Mary He's staring at the fish in those tanks.

Dan Perhaps he wants to eat them.
They remind him of food.

Mary Oh Dan! I think they remind him of his home.
I think they remind him of the SEA.

Mary What did that boy say, Dan?

Dan He said, "That's not an AQUARIUM pet."

Mary It is!
I mean, HE is.

Dan Then the boy asked me where the aquarium is, so I said he's outgrown it.

Mary Yes, Winkie is much too big for the fish tank.

Dan Then the boy said, "He's not a fish, so it's not fair for him to be put in the same class as my fish."

Mary Oh dear! What shall we do?

Dan I know! I'll go and ask Mr Hunter from the Pet Shop. ★

Mary Dan! Dan! What did Mr Hunter say?

Dan He said that he'd talked to the Vicar and ...

Mary Yes? Yes?

Dan ...they'd agreed that there should be a special prize for the most UNUSUAL pet.

Will Winkie win the special prize for the most unusual pet?

8 Well Done, Winkie!

Mr and Mrs Kane are waiting for Dan, Mary and Winkie to come home from the Pet Show.

Dad Just look at the time. It's nearly six o' clock.

Mum It's time they were home, but let's wait a bit longer.

Dad I bet it takes some judges ages to decide which pet deserves a prize.

Mum I hope our Winkie wins something. Dan and Mary would be over the moon if he did.

Dad What about a bit of supper?

Mum It's fish and chips.

Dad ★ Listen! That sounded like the garden gate.

Mum Look out of the window, Dad. It's them.

Dad They're coming up the path. ★ And look! Winkie has got a big, blue rosette hanging round his neck.

Mary Mum! Dad! Look at Winkie!

Dan He got a rosette and fifty pence.

Dad What for ... exactly?

Dan For being the most unusual pet in the whole Show.

Mum Well done Winkie!

45

Dan He was famous! Crowds and crowds of people queued up to see him.

Mary And each one paid ten pence.

Dan Then about fifty people followed him home in the wheelbarrow.

Dad He's getting very big. He won't fit in the wheelbarrow much longer.

Dan He'll soon be the size of a sheep.

Dad People round here are beginning to talk about him, you know.

Mum That Mrs Baker keeps saying, "What is it? What is it?"

Mary What do you tell her, Mum?

Mum I tell her he's a sea lion.

Mary Oh Mum! She can see he's not a sea lion.

Dad You could say he's a RARE kind of sea lion.

Mum And for all we know, he is.

Dan At the rate he's growing, he'll more likely be a rare kind of sea ELEPHANT

Mary I wish he'd stop growing.

Dad You know, Uncle Fred was right. He does look a bit like the Loch Ness Monster..

Dan None of the prehistoric monsters in that library book look quite like Winkie.

Mum If he grows much more, we'll have to take him back to the Pet Shop.

Mary Oh Mum! We can't do that! He's our pet.

Dan He'd be like a bull in a china shop. D'you think she'd give us our money back?

Mary You think you're funny, don't you, Dan Kane?

Dad Come on, all of you. Let's take Winkie into the garden and see how much he's grown today?

Do you think that Winkie will get too big to stay with the Kanes?

9 Trouble for Winkie

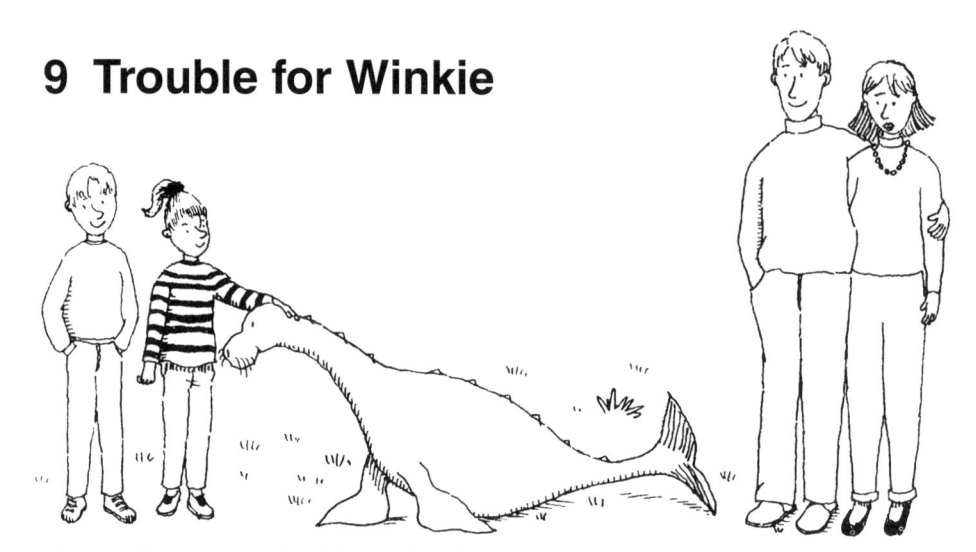

A few days later the Kane family are in the garden again, looking at Winkie.

Mary Oh Winkie! I wish you didn't eat so much.

Dad Look at his eyes, Mary. I think he knows what you're saying. He's very intelligent.

Dan We could train him.

Mum What could we train him for?

Dad We could just teach him simple commands. You know ...SIT... and STAY...

Mary ... and BEG.

Dan He comes to me when I give him my special whistle.

Mum Do it then, Dan.

Dan All right. ★ Look! He's coming.

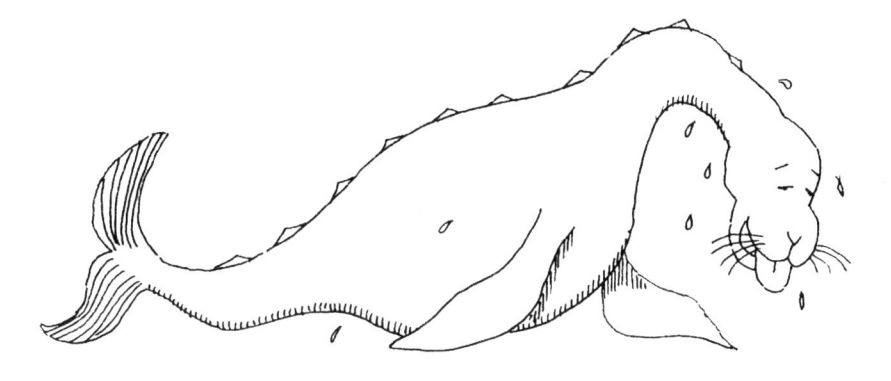

Dad	But he's moving very slowly and ★ he's panting.
Mary	I hope he's not going to be ill.
Mum	He's too hot. We don't want to have to take him to the PDSA.
Dad	I wonder what they would make of him there?
Mum	He's not ill. He's just too hot.
Dan	Well, we've filled his bath about ten times today. But the minute he gets in, it's empty, after a good splash.
Mary	I know! We could take him for a swim.
Dad	Good idea! He'd enjoy that.
Dan	Yes, we could let him go for a swim in the canal at the bottom of the garden.
Mary	Oh yes. Let's do that.
Mum	We'll do it after tea.
Dad	I'll unlock the garden gate, then Winkie can get over the tow path and into the water.

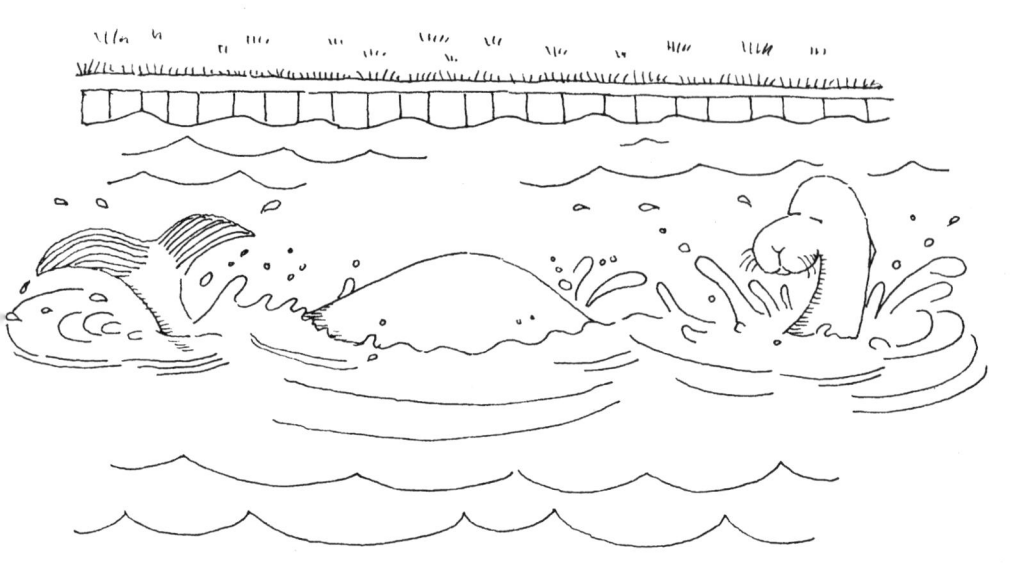

Mary	Look at him! He loves it.
Mum	Look at him ducking and diving ...
Dad	...and throwing back his long neck.
Dan	★ Now he's letting out whoops of excitement.
Dad	Fetch the camera, Dan. Let's get a picture of him.
Dan	OK, I'll get it.★
Mum	There's Mrs Baker from next door. What's she saying, Mary?
Mary	She's saying, "Well I never!"
Dan	"Put him in a circus!"
Dad	Look how he's showing off . . . turning somersaults and diving.

Mum	★ Here's Dan with the camera.
Dad	Winkie's a proper film star. Pity we haven't got a ciné.
Mary	Get one of him doing a nose dive, Dan.★
Dan	I'll get him with his tail left standing up clear out of the water. ★
Dad	He must be tired after doing all that nose diving.
Mary	★ He must be hungry too.
Mum	Yes, he MUST be hungry. I'll go and put out his pail with the scraps in.★
Dan	Look at him! He only has to hear the rattle of a pail and he's there. ★
Dad	Let's go inside and leave him with his nose buried in his food. ★

Mum He had a good splash, didn't he?

Mary He loved it. Dear Winkie!
But I wish he'd stop growing.

Dad Now ... I've been thinking. We'd better all have a good talk about everything.

Mary What do you mean, Dad?

Mum Yes, we've got to have a good talk.

Dan What exactly does that mean?

Dad It's just that we've got to be sensible.

Mum It's hard to know what to do for the best.

Mary We can't let Winkie go.
We can't.

Dan You're not trying to say that Winkie's got to go, are you?

Dad I don't really see how we're going to keep him here. He's eating us out of house and home and look at the size of him.

Mum We just don't know when it's going to stop.

Mary I thought you liked him, Mum.

Mum I do. At least I did when he first came out of the stone egg.

Dan You can't get rid of him. He's a present.

Mary You can't give presents away.

Mum I've still got the real present.

Dad Yes, it's on the shelf.

Mum And it's lovely.

Dan No, the Gift's the real present. Isn't he, Mary?

Mary Yes, he is.
Winkie's the real present.

Will the Kanes have to get rid of Winkie?

10 More Trouble

*A few days later, the Kanes hear a commotion in the garden.★
They all rush to the back door to see what is going on.★*

    Mary   ★ Listen to Winkie!

    Dan   ★ He's making that high, angry yapping sound.

    Dad   Like when you show him a pound of biscuits and then only give him half a dozen.

    Mary   Look! There's Mrs Baker.

    Mum   She's got a yard brush in her hand.

    Dan   ★ Listen to her shrieking!

    Mary   Look at her red face.

    Dad   We must have left the gate open.

    Dan   That's it! She's just slammed it behind Winkie.

    Mum   Oh dear! Oh dear!★ Now she's shouting at Winkie.

Dad Can you hear what she's saying, Dan?

Dan She's saying, "Don't you come back here, you thieving little monster!"

Mary What did Winkie steal?

Dan She says he ate half a row of Mr Baker's cabbages.

Mum Oh dear! What will Mr Baker say?

Dad I can't think how that gate got left open. I'll go and tell Mrs Baker that we're sorry and that it won't happen again. ★

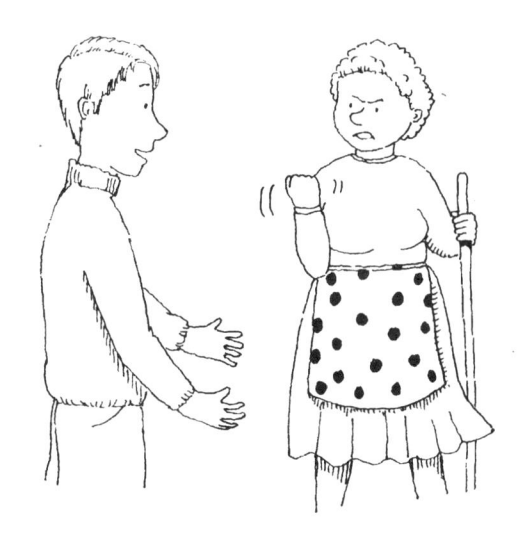

Mum We must make sure that the gate is kept shut.

Dan It's putting temptation in his way. You know what he's like for scraps.

Mary He loves his pail of scraps.

Dan Here's Dad.

Mary What did Mrs Baker say, Dad?

Dad She said that Winkie's grown since yesterday.

Mum That's true.

Dad And she said that it's not natural.

Mary Well, he does eat a lot.

Dad Mrs Baker said that what we've got to be careful of, is that he doesn't go round eating humans!

Mary HUMANS!

Mum You're a bad boy, Winkie! A bad boy!

What will the Kanes do now?

11 A Big Problem

The Kanes are watching Winkie who is gazing over the gate at the canal.

Mary Look at him sitting there!

Dad I do believe he's grown another metre in all directions.

Mum He's as big as a donkey now.

Dan Well! We know he isn't a sea lion now.

Dad Mrs Baker was right. It isn't natural.
Even elephants don't grow that quickly.

Dan Yes, it takes them years to get to that size.
...YEARS.

Dad Uncle Fred says we should hand him over to the PDSA.

Mum They'd see to him. It's their job.

Dan But he's not a stray, Dad.

Mary No, he's our pet.

Dad Uncle Fred says we ought to get him out of here before he gets to his full size.

Mum And what does Uncle Fred reckon that will be?

Dan I suppose he thinks that Winkie will be a Loch Ness monster. That's what he said before.

Dad Mmm! I think Uncle Fred could be right, you know.

Dan Right about what, Dad?

Dad About the PDSA.

Mary Oh Dad!

Dad We'll have to think about it.

Mary I don't want to think about it.

Dan Just thinking about it makes me feel terrible.

Dad It's no good! The PDSA would take him back to where he belongs.

Mum That's right. Look at him now ... panting for water.

Will the Kanes take Winkie to the PDSA so that he can go back to the water where he belongs?

12 Winkie settles it

The next morning Mary runs to her bedroom window to toss down Winkie's early morning biscuits. ★ *She sees an empty garden.*

Mary   Winkie! WINKIE! W I N K I E!

Mum   What's the matter, Mary?

Dad   Come downstairs, Mary, and tell us what's wrong.

Dan   Come on, Mary.★ Hurry! ★

Mary   He's gone ... GONE!

Dan   GONE! He can't have.

Mary   Yes, Winkie's gone.

Dad   She must be right because there's nothing in the garden big enough to hide him.

Dan   Come on! Let's go out and look for clues. ★

Mum Yes, he's gone. But look! The gate's still shut.

Dad I know what's happened. He's jumped over the gate and into the canal. We ought to have known that he'd do it sooner or later.

Mary Oh, Dad!

Dan It's almost as if he's known that we'd talked about getting rid of him.

Dad Well, he must be back in the water now where he belongs.

Mary Oh Dad! He belonged to us.

Mum Perhaps he'll find his way back to the sea.

Dad It could be all for the best.

Mary How can you say that, Dad?

Dan I think that he's splashing his way up the canals, back to his true home in the sea.

Dad Perhaps we shall find him again one day.

Mum Then you could give him your whistle, Dan.

Mary I don't think we shall ever find Winkie again.

Mum Cheer up everybody! After all, we've still got the egg up on the shelf.

Dan And it's the same, except for the brown crack running the length of the bluish green stone.

Do you think the Kanes will ever see Winkie again?

Read: *A Gift from Winklesea*
by Helen Cresswell
published by Hodder Children's Books

Also published

For pupils of 6-8 years ready to move on from the Take Part Starters

Mystery at Winklesea
From an original story by Helen Cresswell

Another story of Dan's and Mary's adventures with their unusual pet.

ISBN 0 7062 5360 4
4 parts for reading ages 6 to 8

Other Recent *Take Part* Series Titles

The Battle of Bubble and Squeak
From an original story by Philippa Pearce

The Whitbread Book Award-winning story about the family battle which ensues when two children agree to look after a friend's pet gerbils.
ISBN 0 7062 5221 7
8 parts for reading ages 7 to 8

The Village Dinosaur
From an original story by Phyllis Arkle

A small boy finds and befriends a living dinosaur buried in the local quarry. This is the story of the hilarious adventures that follow.
ISBN 0 7062 5222 5
8 parts for reading ages 7 to 8

The Adventures of Odysseus
From an original story by
Sheila Lane and Marion Kemp

Odysseus and his crew encounter exciting adventures on the voyage from Troy to Ithaca. The famous characters and events from Greek mythology including the evil Cyclops are brought alive and provide an enjoyable way to learn about Greek myth and legend.

ISBN 0 7062 5225 X
4 main parts plus 2 for each of 3 stories, for reading ages 7 to 9

A Story of King Arthur
An original story by
Sheila Lane and Marion Kemp

In the Dark Ages, when knights were waiting for a new king to lead them in battles against Saxon invaders, Mordred the Evil One is determined to make her son king.

ISBN 0 7062 5305 1
7 parts, for reading ages 7 to 9

Christopher Columbus

An original story by
Sheila Lane and Marion Kemp

Adventures on the seas, near-mutiny, diseases and the discovery of the New World provide reading excitement and learning.

ISBN 0 7062 5224 1
8 parts for reading ages 7 to 9

The Riddle Girl
An original story by
Sheila Lane

A tale set in Anglo Saxon times. A poor family's valuable herd of pigs has gone missing, stolen by the village chief's son. To get them back, the family's young daughter has to make up a riddle that the chief cannot answer.

ISBN 0 7062 5224 1
8 parts for reading ages 7 to 9

All Aboard the Ark
An original story by
Sheila Lane and Marion Kemp

A group of friends, Elephant, Camel, Giraffe, Monkey, Rabbit and Tortoise manage to stowaway on the Ark when the rains come..

ISBN 0 7062 5304 3
6 parts for reading ages 6 to 9

THE TAKE PART HANDBOOK
A Resource book for teachers

An English programme using the *Take Part* series for Key Stages One and Two of the National Curriculum.

The *Take Part* Handbook consists of:

* A number of units, or chapters, based on specific Take Part books
* The first unit helps children develop the skills they need to use Take Part Books successfully. This unit also helps those teachers unfamiliar with the Take Part series.
* 25 Mastersheets for pupils